D1085296

That's Just Spooky!

EXTREME MONSTER STORIES

Thomas Kingsley Troupe

BLACK
RABBIT
BOOKS

Hi Jinx is published by Black Rabbit Books
P.O. Box 3263, Mankato, Minnesota, 56002.
www.blackrabbitbooks.com
Copyright © 2019 Black Rabbit Books

Jennifer Besel, editor; Michael Sellner, designer;
Catherine Cates, production designer;
Omay Ayres, photo researcher

All rights reserved. No part of this book may
be reproduced in any form without written
permission from the publisher.

Library of Congress Cataloging-in-Publication Data
Names: Troupe, Thomas Kingsley, author.
Title: Extreme monster stories / by Thomas Kingsley Troupe.
Description: Mankato, Minnesota : Black Rabbit Books, 2019. |
Series: Hi jinx. That's just spooky! | Includes bibliographical
references and index. |
Audience: Ages 9-12. | Audience: Grades 4 to 6.
Identifiers: LCCN 2017061645| ISBN 9781680726350
(library binding) | ISBN 9781680727654 (pbk.) |
ISBN 9781680726411 (e-book)
Subjects: LCSH: Monsters—Juvenile literature.
Classification: LCC GR825 .T695 2019 | DDC 001.944—dc23
LC record available at https://lccn.loc.gov/201706164

Printed in the United States. 5/18

Image Credits

Alamy: Chronicle, 20 (inset); Science History Images, 3 (bkgd); AP Images:
Jeff Gentner, 6–7 (mothman); commons.wikimedia.org: 19 (monster);
Dreamstime: Microvone, Back Cover, 1, 21 (bkgd); iStock: RichVintage, 16
(Bigfoot); Science Source: Jaime Chirinos, 10–11 (monster); Shutterstock:
Cat_arch_angel, 14 (bkgd); Christos Georghiou, 4–5 (claws), 14–15 (wolf);
DenisKrivoy, 15 (bkgd); Gervanio, 12–13 (wheel); Jamesbin, 12–13 (hands);
jannoon028, 6, 9, 10, 12, 14, 17, 18 (note card); Joe Prachatree, 12–13 (girl);
jumpingsack, 6–7 (bkgd); Lightspring, 2–3 (arm), 20 (hand), 21 (foot),
22; Lukiyanova Natalia frenta, Cover, 4 (woods); Memo Angeles, 16 (dog
& lines); Michael Rosskothen, 8–9 (monster); opicobello, 6 (torn paper);
Pasko Maksim, Back Cover, 19, 23, 24 (torn paper); Pitju, 11, 15, 21 (curled
paper); Plus69, Cover, 4 (eyes); Rakchai Duangdee, 12–13 (bkgd); rogistok,
16 (woman); Ron Dale, 5, 6, 20 (marker stroke); Ron Leishman, 15 (deer);
Valentyna Chukhlyebova, 6–7 (wings); wawritto, Cover (hands); yukipon,
10–11 (blood) Every effort has been made to contact copyright holders
for material reproduced in this book. Any omissions will be rectified in
subsequent printings if notice is given to the publisher.

CONTENTS

Chapter 1

A MONSTER TALE

Something **lurks** in the bushes. Its red eyes shine in the dark. You run, but you can hear it coming. Your heart pounds.

Monster stories send **shivers** up the spine. Sink your teeth into these stories before YOU become breakfast!

Chapter 2

STORIES FROM AROUND THE WORLD

Witnesses: several residents

Location: Point Pleasant, West Virginia, United States

Date: 1966–1967

Two couples were driving together by an old factory. All of a sudden, they saw a huge winged creature. They sped away. But the creature flew behind their car. It had glowing eyes and a 10-foot (3-meter) wingspan.

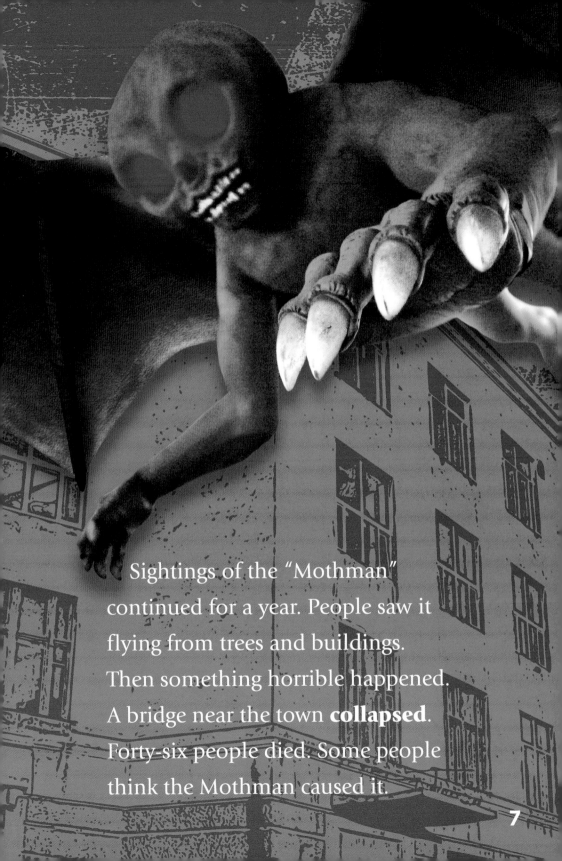

Sightings of the "Mothman"
continued for a year. People saw it
flying from trees and buildings.
Then something horrible happened.
A bridge near the town **collapsed**.
Forty-six people died. Some people
think the Mothman caused it.

The Labynkyr Devil is thought to be about 30 feet (9 m) long. Some think the creature is a plesiosaur.

Devil of the Lake

Witnesses: many residents
Location: Lake Labynkyr, Siberia, Russia
Date: first reported in the 1800s

A cold wind whips across the waters of Siberia's Lake Labynkyr. A dark shape pokes above the surface. Then it disappears again. The creature is known as the Labynkyr Devil. Many people compare it to the Loch Ness Monster.

Scientists are trying to prove the Labynkyr Devil **exists**. A dive team explored the cold lake. Another group used **sonar**. That group found a large shape members can't identify.

El Chupacabra

Witnesses: many people

Location: Puerto Rico, Chile, Brazil, United States, and other places around the world

Date: first reported in the 1960s

El chupacabra is a monster out for blood! It is said to leave a trail of dead animals behind it. Witnesses say it has a reptilelike body and bulging red eyes.

Stories say the creature is like a vampire. It sucks blood from goats, **cattle**, and other animals. But it leaves all the meat behind. No photos of the creature exist. No footprints have been found.

Chupacabra comes from Spanish words that mean "goat sucker."

Witness: Brian Bethel

Location: Abilene, Texas, United States

Date: 1996

Brian Bethel was in his car. There was a sudden knock on his car window. Two boys stood outside. They asked Bethel for a ride.

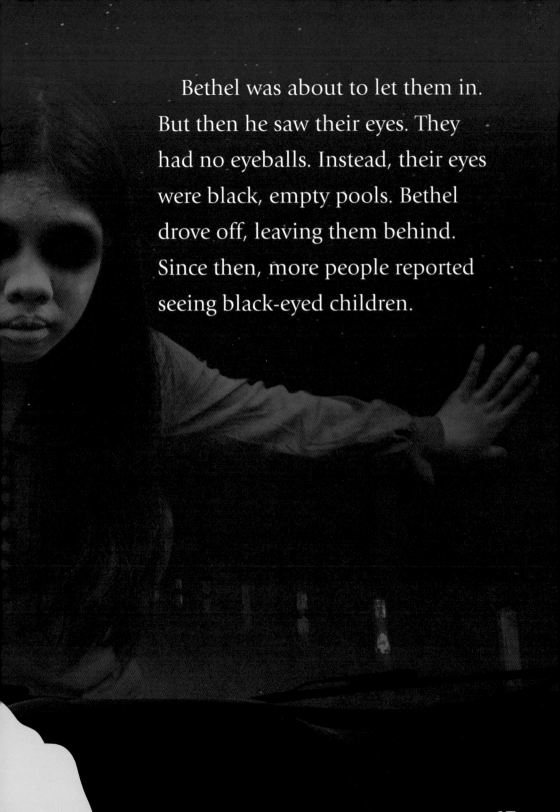

Bethel was about to let them in. But then he saw their eyes. They had no eyeballs. Instead, their eyes were black, empty pools. Bethel drove off, leaving them behind. Since then, more people reported seeing black-eyed children.

The Dogman

Witnesses: many residents

Location: Pennsylvania, Michigan, and Wisconsin in the United States

Date: reports started in the 1800s

Some states are full of stories of the dogman. Witnesses say the monster is a large, hairy beast. It has a long nose and glowing eyes. Some reports say the monster eats deer and leaves the smell of wet dog behind.

The dogman is said to be about 7 feet (2 m) tall.

Bigfoot and Some Puppies

Witness: unnamed
Location: Hocking County, Ohio, United States
Date: August 29, 2011

No book about monsters is complete without a Bigfoot story. These huge creatures are said to roam the forests. One story comes from a woman in Ohio. She said she took her puppies outside. Near the woods, she heard a whistle. The woman whistled back and heard the noise again.

Some branches rustled nearby, and one of her dogs barked. When she looked up, she saw a tall, hairy creature. When the monster saw her, it stepped back into the trees and disappeared.

The Dover Demon

Witnesses: Bill Bartlett and other residents

Location: Dover, Massachusetts, United States

Date: reports started in April 1977

Teenager Bill Bartlett was driving. He caught something in his headlights. A creature on all fours was on a wall. He said it had a baby's body and long arms and legs. It had a watermelon-shaped head and glowing eyes.

The next day, more people reported seeing the "Dover Demon." All of the descriptions matched what Bartlett saw.

The Dover Demon is little. The monster didn't appear to stand more than 4 feet (1 m) tall.

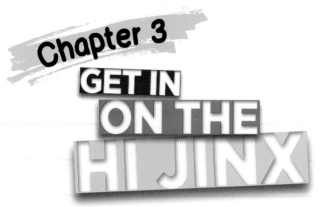

Chapter 3

GET IN ON THE HI JINX

Cryptozoologists are people who study mysterious creatures. They travel to places where strange creatures are reported. They work to find out if the monsters are real. Maybe one day you can be one of these researchers.

The world is a big place. Could it be full of strange monsters? The thought is just spooky!

Take It One Step More

1. Do you think there are monsters in the world? Explain why or why not.

2. If you saw a monster, would you report it? Why or why not?

3. Researchers try to get pictures or videos of monsters. But no one has been able to get good, clear pictures of any monsters. Why do you think they can't?

GLOSSARY

cattle (KAH-tuhl)—cows kept on a farm or ranch

collapse (kuh-LAPS)—to fall or break down completely

exist (ig-ZIST)—to be real or have life

lurk (LURK)—to secretly wait in a place for an evil purpose

plesiosaur (PLEE-see-uh-sohr)—a prehistoric meat-eating marine reptile

resident (REH-zuh-dent)—a person who lives in a place

shiver (SHI-vuhr)—to tremble

sonar (SOH-nar)—a device that uses sound waves to find objects underwater

BOOKS

Bougie, Matt. *Bigfoot, the Loch Ness Monster, and Unexplained Creatures.* Paranormal Investigations. New York: Cavendish Square Publishing, 2017.

Niver, Heather Moore. *Investigating Bigfoot, the Loch Ness Monsters, and Other Cryptids.* Understanding the Paranormal. New York: Britannica Educational Publishing, 2016.

Noll, Elizabeth. *Bigfoot.* Strange … But True? Mankato, MN: Black Rabbit Books, 2017.

WEBSITES

The Bigfoot Field Researchers Organization
bfro.net

The Legend of Loch Ness
www.pbs.org/wgbh/nova/ancient/ legend-loch-ness.html

The Science Behind Bigfoot and Other Monsters
news.nationalgeographic.com/ news/2013/09/130907-cryptid-crytozoology- bigfoot-loch-yeti-monster-abominable-science/

INDEX